PRISCILLA'S MIRACLE

George and Linda B

ISBN (Paperback): 979-8-9891177-2-7
ISBN (Hardbound): 979-8-9891177-3-4
ISBN (eBook): 979-8-9891177-1-0

Priscilla's Miracles

Third Book of the Children's Trilogy

Priscilla had a dream in which she saw her Aunt Dora and Grandfather Smyth distressed as they approached an unfamiliar church. Lightning flashed, and Cilla knew something unexpected and frightening was about to happen. Several weeks later, Priscilla's life and the life of her new family were turned upside down.

Priscilla, Cilla for short, was reading one of the books from her grandfather's library. She was having a good day. Her friends were coming up to her window and saying hello and asking when she could come out to see them. They were sad because they had not seen her for a few weeks.

Dora, Priscilla's aunt, had moved her wheelchair so she had the best light to read.

Cilla was pain free for the first time in many days. Her left arm and leg were totally numb, and she could not move them; however, her right leg and arm were almost normal in feelings, and her ability to move them was improving. She was able to hold the book with her right hand, and she could prop it up on her right knee. Her head sometimes ached, but at least her eyes were clear and focused. She tired easily, but her energy was greatly improved. A new family doctor was coming over after lunch. She hoped she and her Aunt Dora would like Doctor Shultz's replacement.

The seven-year old was supposed to have started school last fall, but the accident had stopped that. Grandfather Smyth was now living again in the house with his daughter Dora and his injured granddaughter. He said it was easier for him to prepare for his lectures while using his library in Dora's home and it was easier to take care of the household and details regarding Priscilla's recovery.

Both Dora and her grandfather were constantly attending to Cilla. Though she missed her parents, her bond with her new family was growing deeper and deeper. She knew she was at home once more. She would never doubt again that she was loved and cared for.

Priscilla had lived in the large Victorian home for over a year now. When she arrived, she had never seen such a large house. Her parents and younger brother had died suddenly from the flu, and she had to leave the farm she loved and all her animal friends to come live with her aunt, who was her mother's younger and only sister.

Dora had been engaged to be married to a bachelor from her church, but complications had ended the relationship many months ago; however, she was still the prettiest and most sought-after eligible young woman in the county. Cilla was determined more than ever to match her up with the best husband possible. Why?

You see, Priscilla and her friends were the reason the first engagement failed. While she knew she had done the correct thing, she still felt an obligation to make things right if she could.

Unknown to Cilla, her yard friends were holding a meeting to discuss what to do to help her recover from her injuries. Sir Boss, the regal squirrel, convened the meeting and asked Sid and his wife to make proposals on what they could do to help. Sid, the tiny man with the crazy white hair, runs the bird riding academy and spoke first.

He said, "This is what we know. Priscilla was riding with her grandfather in his automobile when they were hit by a truck. Priscilla struck her head on the side of the vehicle and was in a coma for several days. When she awoke, she had no feelings in most of her body. However, as the weeks passed, she recovered feelings and movement to her right side, but since then, there had been no progress. Her grandfather was most upset and blamed himself for Cilla's injuries which looked like they would be permanent. The family physician felt it was most likely the young girl would never walk again."

Priscilla's grandfather, the law professor and dean of a nationally respected law school, had turned away from studying the Bible, praying, and attending church. He blamed God for taking his oldest daughter and his only grandson from him. He had immersed himself in study and lecture preparation continuously and had all but ignored Priscilla until she helped him rid his yard of yellowjackets last year. Before the accident, he was beginning to truly bond with his only granddaughter and heal from the loss of his oldest daughter. However, when the car accident almost took Priscilla, his anger returned.

Since the accident, however, Priscilla talked to him about God often and asked that he pray for her recovery. He was most resistant but finally relented. The proud professor could not believe the God who took his oldest daughter would help Priscilla recover.

Despite his misgivings, he started to read the Bible once more and again approached God in prayer. He even started to attend church with Dora. He felt if Priscilla could trust God after she had lost her mother, father, brother, and her ability to walk, who was he to turn away from God!

Professor Smyth joined with Dora to pray for Priscilla's full recovery. He didn't know how or when things would change, but in his heart, he believed it would.

"What can we do to help?" Wanda, the bee rider commander, said loudly, "Her sitting in that chair with wheels and lying in the bed all day is not going to help; we need to get her into the yard and moving. We must figure out a way to free her from the house so she can get some exercise."

The yard physician developed an activity plan for their injured friend. He had it written on a clipboard and was eager to start her treatment as soon as possible.

Just after the accident, Cilla had many dreams and visions. One night, her favorite painting of the lion and the lamb lying down together grew to an enormous size, and an angel appeared. Priscilla was told she would recover completely; however, the healing process would be long and difficult, but her family's healing would be even more miraculous.

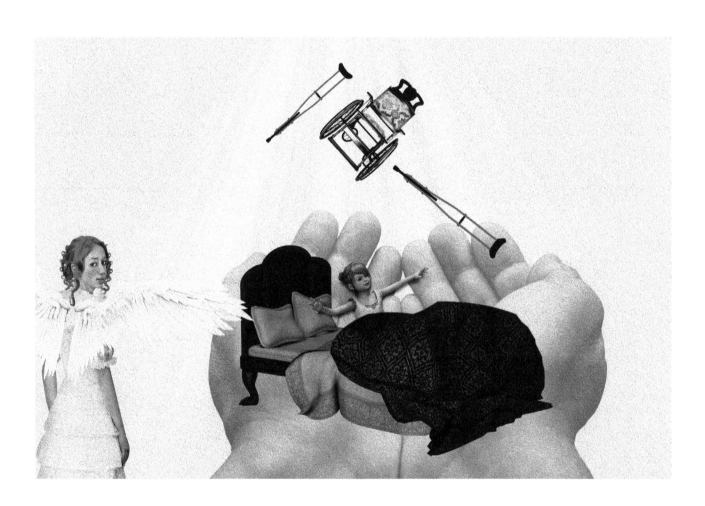

She was told her new family would become closer than ever before and her aunt would find her husband to be, while her grandfather would forgive himself for the accident that injured Priscilla, and they would have many joyful years together as she grew up.

As the long meeting among the yard friends continued, Doctor Daniel Edward Shultz, having recently taken over his father's practice, arrived at Dora's front door. Dora had gone to school with Daniel when they were very young but had not seen him in over fifteen years.

Daniel introduced himself and asked to see Priscilla. Dora was shocked at how handsome he was and how interested he was in helping Priscilla recover. His father told Cilla to stay in bed or in the wheelchair and get as much rest as possible. He limited her physical movement and forbade her to go outside. The young doctor disagreed with his father's old school approach and wanted Priscilla to get as much sunshine and exercise as she wanted.

He continued, "I know my father doesn't think Cilla will ever regain her ability to walk and be normal again. He thinks this is so because of the long length of time her left side has gone without feelings, nor has she been able to use her muscles on that side either. I disagree and wish to try several new things. Will you allow me to try?"

Dora responded, "Let me talk to my father. He trusted your father in these matters, and we will have you return after we have talked."

Later that day, Sid came to Cilla's window while Dora was busy working on her oil painting.

He brought Olie Owl and talked to Priscilla about what the yard committee had decided to do to help the injured young girl recover. He briefed Cilla, "We decided to treat you for your injuries and need to shrink you so Olie can fly you down to the pond in your wheel-chair. Don't panic; we have it all under control." Cilla thought for a moment and was so very eager to get out of the house she would agree to almost anything.

She said with glee, "Yes, please. Let's go while Dora is busy painting!"

Sid shrunk Cilla down to such a small size that Olie could pick her up with his talons and fly her to the pond.

They soared through the open window and were within seconds flying over the pond above the pink water lily blooms. The young flyer had no idea what was going to happen next.

Suddenly, Olie dropped the wheelchair and Cilla in one motion. The screaming young girl went headfirst into the water below. The water was colder than she remembered, and the shock was breathtaking.

Within seconds, Twig the pond creature swam to Priscilla and told her to hang on to the shell on his back. She grabbed with her right hand, the only hand that worked, and held on for dear life. Cilla felt the cold water on her left side, and she yelled, "I can feel the cold water with my left hand and leg!" She was amazed and was crying with joy.

Twig with Cilla on his back swam over to where the yard doctor was standing. Wanda and other nymph warriors tied Cilla's legs, arms, and hands to Twig's back, arms, legs, and hands. So, every time Twig moved, Cilla also moved the same way. They swam like this for quite some time.

By the time Cilla was getting very tired and cold, the doctor yelled, "It is time to get Cilla dried off and back into her wheelchair to fly back to the house!" The process was reversed, and Cilla returned through the window, and Sid enlarged her to her normal size. They did this every day and completed several weeks before the new young doctor made his first official visit to see Priscilla.

Later that month, the handsome young doctor came to see Priscilla. He had with him a set of crutches.

He said, "Cilla, I am your new doctor, and I am taking over from my father. I have talked to your Aunt Dora and Grandfather Smyth; we are going to change your treatment. We are going to get you out of that wheelchair as much as you are able and teach you how to move with a pair of crutches. We will start today if you are willing?"

Cilla, excited, almost yelled, "Yes, of course, let's get started!"

Priscilla was much stronger than the good doctor imagined. She was already getting some muscle tone in her left side. She was able to stand and move the crutch to her right side and take a few halting steps. She could not use two crutches because she did not have enough strength in her left side yet.

He asked her, "Have you been doing some exercising? You have much better strength than I thought possible. Do you have feelings in your left arm, hand, and leg?"

Cilla took a long time to answer but was unable to lie, "Yes, I do have some feeling in my left side. I cannot grasp anything in my left hand, but I have some movement in my left arm and leg. Please don't tell Aunt Dora. I want to surprise her and Grandfather Smyth."

He smiled and said, "Alright, this is our little secret. When you are ready, we will show your family your amazing progress. But can you tell me how you have accomplished so much?"

Cilla asked the doctor, "Can you keep a secret? If you can, I will show you something you won't understand; it is a miracle."

The young man had been warned about Cilla's vivid imagination, but he could not resist the offer. "Sure, please show me."

Priscilla told him, "Push me in my chair down to the edge of the pond." As they went to the water, Cilla explained, "My progress you see is because I swim every day in the pond. I have many friends in the yard, and they help me with my therapy." The doctor smiled and tried not to giggle. He in no way wanted to discourage the young girl's fantasy. Obviously, whatever she was doing was working. A positive mental outlook, he knew, was very important in healing anyone.

Sid, Wanda, and the yard doctor rushed in from the shrubs to the right of where Cilla and the doctor stopped at the edge of the pond. Sid shrunk Cilla and the doctor immediately. Twig swam up to the edge, and Cilla slid out of her wheelchair and got on Twig's back. Priscilla's doctor was dumbfounded; he could not believe what he was seeing. The yard doctor asked Dr. Shultz if he would like to see the treatment plan on his clipboard. He said, "As you can see, Priscilla is making excellent progress. We have documented thirty hours of water exercise this month. I see a definite improvement in her strength, balance, and movement. If she continues to progress at this pace, I predict she will be walking without crutches or other support within four months."

After Cilla completed her swimming, she returned to the wheelchair. The young doctor pushed Cilla from the pond back to the house. To the doctor's delight, several of Priscilla's friends hitched a ride, including the yard doctor. Dr. Shultz was just beginning to appreciate what he was seeing.

Cilla addressed the blank-faced adult, "I think you are in shock; however, I promise you, this is real. By the way, do you like Dora?" The young doctor stammered; the question was completely unexpected.

He answered, "Well, well, I guess so."

"Dora was someone I adored, from the first time I met her twenty years ago."

"Good! It is time you bring her some flowers and ask her out for a nice meal," Priscilla exclaimed. "So, before you leave today, ask her if you can return to talk to her about my progress."

He responded, "After what I witnessed today, how could I refuse to do what you have asked? Not only that, but it is also exactly what I wanted to do since I saw her once again."

Aunt Dora came in to tuck Cilla into bed and got in with her to spend some time before going to bed herself.

Priscilla, not wanting to miss an opportunity, asked, "Aunt Dora, do you like Doctor Shultz? He sure is good looking, don't you think? I bet he likes you a lot and wants to ask you out."

Dora, a bit embarrassed by Priscilla's questions and enthusiasm, reluctantly responded, "Don't you think those are several personal questions I might not want to share with you at this time? However, he did talk to me about you and was so very pleased with your progress. He also asked me if he could come by some evening to spend time with your grandfather and me."

Excited Cilla exclaimed, "You accepted, right?"

Dora returned her excitement, "Yes, I did, and he is coming over tomorrow evening! Now, are you happy?"

Dr. Shultz came over that night and brought some flowers. Dora was very pleased with his attention and spent hours talking about their school days as well as how Priscilla was progressing. Dora remembered Daniel Edward Shultz but never considered him as a boy-friend when they were children.

She thought, *Wow! How things had changed*. When she broke up with her fiancé last year, she never imagined someone would come into her life this quickly. Priscilla had become the center of her life, and now she thought she had found someone who could share her care of Priscilla in a way no one except her father could.

Months later, after hours and hours of water therapy and other treatments, Priscilla stood by Dora as she and Dr. Shultz got married. Cilla walked into the church without wheelchair or crutches. She was the flower girl. It was a wonderful day for everyone including Professor Smyth. His daughter was getting married, and his granddaughter was a normal healthy young girl. He thanked God for all his many blessings!

Many of the yard friends watched the ceremony from the rafter in the ceiling of the church.

The End.

ABOUT THE AUTHORS

The author George B is an avid photographer and graphic designer. He retired as a senior scientist and shares his writing passion with his wife of forty-four years.

Linda B, the coauthor, is a teacher, registered nurse, and an accomplished musician. She teaches piano and plays for churches.

Our creative efforts are found in two previous children's books, *Priscilla's Prayer*, *Priscilla's Angels*, and now, in our third book, *Priscilla's Miracle*. We have published two previous books written for older audiences: *Struggle and Survival: A Boneyard Saga, Short Story Anthology* and *Volume 1, Mona Lisa on the Moon, Thirty-Two Thousand Years in the Making*.

BOOK DEDICATION

This book was inspired by and is dedicated to Barbara (Rose) Santora. Barbara is recovering from a devastating stroke. Her courage, determination, and spirit parallels Priscilla's journey in so many ways.

Printed in the USA
CPSIA information can be obtained
at www.ICGtesting.com
LVHW061818311023
762647LV00011B/44